You Can Choose

--

Life is Complicated, But the Universe is Really Simple

PETER BOSTWICK

&

BETH BOSTWICK

DEDICATION

This book is dedicated to our family, friends, choosers and fellow explorers.

CONTENTS

INTRODUCTION

+++

Who is this book for?

If you are at a point in your life where you are open to considering different approaches to living a more fulfilling life, this book is for you. This is not a 'how to' book. It's a book to help you think about **you** and how **you** interact with the world.

By taking the time to ponder the material in this book, you will begin to understand the power of your thinking, and why it's so important to create the life you want to live.

Peter and I have lived a life made up of a variety of experiences, some good, some not so good. Given the shared travels we've had over 30+ years of marriage, we've learned a great deal about each other and have grown in many different ways. In particular, we have begun to understand the power of thoughts and how beliefs and feelings impact our lives.

In this book, we have put together simple, stand-alone chapters that reflect the evolution of our thinking. It's like a CliffsNotes™ version of many other writings.

We wrote the book so you can read a chapter each week and reflect on what it says to you. You can read it through in one sitting, but you'll miss the benefit of thinking about the various topics as they relate to you.

There is so much useful information written about the law of attraction, the power of the mind, and metaphysics, but some of it is so difficult to read and understand. YouTube helps, but sometimes the videos are complex, repetitive, and don't offer any real help. We wanted to put together a short, accessible book that captures the essence contained in many of the great teachings.

If you are already familiar with these concepts, the chapters will remind you of what you already know and maybe practice.

If the concepts are new to you, hopefully, this book will encourage you to read more and continue your journey beyond reading this book.

One of the fundamental principles of the *You Can Choose* philosophy is that we have individual choice. We believe each of us has choices and we get to live a full life based on those choices.

Another principle of *You Can Choose* is that each of us is so much greater than who we think we are.

We are each an extension of the Universe and have multiple levels of awareness. We have access to these multiple levels through our Greater-Self. Our physical, or Active-Self, is just the tip of who we really are.

The world revolves around our thoughts, beliefs, and feelings. Nothing ever just happens to us; all that we experience is a reflection of ourselves. Our body, our relationships, the circumstances of our lives, are all an extension of how we think, believe and feel about ourselves.

The wonderful part is *we can choose the way we think*. With a little bit of practice and understanding, we can begin to choose our thoughts, beliefs, and feelings and create the world we want — a world of abundance, joy, and adventure that is of our choosing.

If we flip the coin to the other side, we can't blame others. Nothing happens unless we create it; it's all on us as individuals. It is another reason why understanding our thoughts is so important.

It can be scary to think we are each responsible for ourselves, but it is also very liberating. You can create the life you want for yourself, all by yourself – no assistance needed from others.

+++

SECTION 1

+++

HANDBOOK ON LIFE

+++

One of the most fundamental concepts in this book is the power of our beliefs. Beliefs influence everything in our lives, from how we interpret people and events to our ability to manipulate the world.

Beliefs are like rules. They are agreements we've made with ourselves to make living easier. They allow us to deal with what is right in front of us without having to spend time relearning the details of every situation. Our set of beliefs is like a handbook we established many years ago that regulates what we think we should and should not do. We established many of the rules with our families before we knew we were adding them to our handbook.

Like most handbooks, we rarely take the time to go through our beliefs to make sure the rules and policies still apply. At one time, it made sense to check with an authority figure (like mom) before we crossed the street, but as an adult, asking for permission may no longer make sense.

Just like a handbook, our beliefs are available to us if we take the time to look.

We hope you will crack open your handbook to see which beliefs you like and which no longer apply. We hope you will gain the knowledge and confidence to change the ones that no longer have a purpose or meaning for you.

CONGRATULATIONS

+++

Congratulations!

You've been doing this without effort your entire life.

You don't have to understand how it happens or even the role you play to make it happen.

While some of the concepts in this book may be new to you, you are already an expert at using your thoughts, beliefs, and feelings to create your world.

Most of us go through life not realizing what we think about matters, that our beliefs are fundamental, or that our feelings hold so much information. We don't recognize our body and our world are reflections of our thoughts, beliefs, and feelings.

The idea behind this book is to introduce some fundamental ideas about how the universe works, and most importantly, show you how powerful you are.

You are already using all the concepts in this book. We want to show you how to create with purpose and intentionally make choices in your life through your thinking.

You can choose what you think, what you believe, and how you react to your feelings, and then will begin to see it realized in your life.

YOU THINK

+++

Descartes said it succinctly with his famous quote,

"I think, therefore I am."

We all think. We think all the time. We sit and think about the future, and we think about the past. We wonder about the opportunities we have and those we passed up. While watching TV, we think about what we see, how someone looks or who the bad guy is.

We can't help thinking. It's what makes us who we are. We are thinking creatures.

Our mind is by far our most powerful tool. With it, we imagine and create everything we see and experience.

Like any tool, if used properly, our mind can do wonderful things. If properly tuned, it can far exceed our expectations.

The types of thoughts we have are based on our beliefs. Our beliefs reinforce our thoughts.

It's circular logic: the more we think about certain things, and in certain ways, the more our beliefs are reinforced, which causes us to continue to think the same type of thoughts. This powerful, reinforcing phenomena is why so many people stay where they are in life, making the same mistakes.

YOUR THOUGHTS MATTER AND YOU CAN CHOOSE YOUR THOUGHTS

Your thoughts matter because they are how you interpret the world. As you see and experience life, you form thoughts which become opinions and eventually beliefs.

Your beliefs, in turn greatly influence your thoughts.

While it's the beliefs that you ultimately want to understand, you get to your beliefs through your thoughts.

Through the power of your thoughts, you chose to read this book. Based on your thoughts, you will choose the next steps you take on your life's adventure.

Your choices matter and each choice starts with a thought.

You get to choose, and it starts with your thoughts.

YOU CAN CHOOSE EVERYTHING

Life is all about choices. You simply can't do everything at the same time. With your choices, you can live an automatic life or an intentional one.

How much influence do we have with our choices? In other words, does it really matter what we choose?

The answer is YES!

We influence everything we experience. Nothing happens by accident. We do so by the choices we make through our thoughts, beliefs, and feelings.

As we go through our day, many of our choices are automatic. We don't even recognize them as choices. When we get in the car, we automatically put on our seatbelt and start it up. We don't recognize that each and every movement what we give our attention to is a choice.

To live an intentional life, we get to make intentional choices.

LOVE IS UNIVERSAL

+++

Love is the most powerful and ubiquitous energy in the universe.

Love is in and of everything. It bubbles to the top as soon as we allow it. You can think of it as the air that permeates all. Not just surrounding all, but infusing all as well.

Love, like all energy, can be multiplied, accelerated, and shared without limit.

You can refuse and cut off love as easily as you can refuse the air you breathe with equally damaging results.

We naturally want to breathe, and we naturally want to love.

THERE IS NO JUDGEMENT

+++

The Universe offers us love and non-judgmental support. It wants us to succeed without an opinion of how we define success.

As we live our life, we have the opportunity to define success.

If you want to become rich and powerful and have the thoughts, beliefs, and feelings to make that happen, the Universe is fully supportive.

If we dislike ourselves or think the world is out to get us, the Universe will help us achieve that reality as well.

Just like when a mother thinks her child can do no wrong and offers every form of love and assistance for them to succeed, the Universe does the same for us.

The great thing about all this is that you can choose. You can choose what you want, and the Universe will help you achieve it.

There is no judgment from the Universe, but rather unconditional love, acceptance, and support.

+++

SECTION 2

+++

IT'S ALL ABOUT YOU

+++

We are told throughout our life to think of others or not to be selfish. We are frequently reminded that what other people think and do is more important than what we think and do.

Nothing and nobody is more important than you.

Everything you see and experience is from your perspective. You are the center of your Universe.

We are not suggesting that you ignore others or that others are not important. They are important.

However, the only person you can be is you. You should be your focus.

Take care of yourself first. Everything in your life builds from how you see and take care of yourself.

You have the power and opportunity to be who you are and who you choose to become.

Only when you become more you, can you reach out and truly help others.

LOVE YOURSELF

+++

It is important to love yourself - to unconditionally love yourself.

You are unique and an extension of the Universe. You are an integral part of everything.

By loving yourself, you bring positive, reinforcing energy to your whole being. When you reinforce your creative potential, you are able to live a more meaningful and fulfilling life.

The unconditional part of self-love is crucial.

You will make mistakes. You will make choices and have interactions you wish you hadn't. Those are just choices and interactions. They are not you. You remain this wonderful being expressing your creativity.

We are usually our harshest critic. We can easily find and emphasis our faults and discount and ignore our many strengths. We can easily dismiss compliments whereby denying the power that good feelings can bring us.

Instead, be open to loving yourself. You are still you, regardless of what you do.

YOU ARE WHO YOU THINK YOU ARE

+++

If you think you are poor or shy, then you will conform your body and behaviors to reflect that. If you think you are boring, you will broadcast that message out to those around you, "I'm boring."

Most of us don't challenge who we are. We've readily accepted the labels others have given us. Maybe we are the same or the opposite of our parents.

No matter what you look like or what you say or do, if you think you are something, that's the message you send out to others.

You can be who you want to be by focusing on how you think of yourself. Think of yourself in the way you want others to see you.

You've spent most of your life thinking of yourself a certain way. Can you see how the thoughts you've had about yourself are reflected in how others see you?

YOUR WHOLE SELF

+++

The physical you that you know so well is just a tiny portion of the whole you. The physical you is driven mostly by your ego to deal with the day-to-day tasks of living in the world.

When we say *You Can Choose*, we don't mean just the you that you point to, but the whole you. We call this 'whole you' the Whole-Self.

Your Whole-Self is made up of three 'selves.'

The <u>Active-Self</u> is the self that is most familiar. This is the self that talks, walks, and thinks. It is often referred to as the ego self.

The <u>Believing-Self</u> is the self that is just below the surface. The Believing-Self keeps track of all the rules, patterns, stories and beliefs to deal with life.

The <u>Greater-Self</u> is at a far different level – it is much more expansive and all-encompassing, almost god-like. It's still you, but with a much larger perspective.

We use the analogy of a tree. Like all analogies, it's not perfect, but it can bring some clarity, and it will be useful as we continue to describe the Whole-Self in more detail.

GREATER-SELF

Think of the root system of the tree as the Greater-Self. Like the roots of a tree, you don't see them and usually pay little attention to them, but they provide nourishment, the base foundation and general direction for the tree. Our Greater-Self provides the same for us.

BELIEVING-SELF

The trunk and branches of the tree represent the Believing-Self. The branches and trunk of a tree grow stronger over time and are slow to change. Your beliefs, like the trunk and branches of a tree, provide form and structure to your thoughts and the type of life experiences you have during your lifetime.

ACTIVE-SELF

The leaves are like your Active-Self. When you look at a tree, you first see the leaves. The leaves come and go but are just as vital to the tree as they guide the tree's growth by providing energy through the conversion of sunshine. You can tell the type, health, and vigor of a tree by simply inspecting the leaves.

All parts of the tree are essential. The leaves, branches, and roots all work in unison for the tree to thrive, just as all three Selves work together for you. You can't have a tree without some type of root system, branches, and leaves.

All three of our Selves – the Greater-Self, the Believing-Self, and the Active-Self are involved when you make choices throughout your lifetime. It's your Whole-Self that creates your uniqueness and directs the life you lead.

YOU ARE ENOUGH

+++

When we say, 'I've had enough' it usually means I've had more than I want.

Since most of us have grown up in this commercial society, we are taught to want more. We constantly compare ourselves with others and often find ourselves lacking. We're not enough.

We have expectations as well. We want things to turn out our way, with steps we've chosen and our preferred result. Not meeting our own expectations, is another example of not enough.

When we think we have enough, there is no gap between our present physical and mental situation. When we are satisfied, we have enough.

By knowing and accepting yourself and your present situation as enough, you open yourself up to move forward in whatever direction you choose.

YOU PICKED YOU

+++

Your body was custom designed just for you to help you with your life experiences and challenges.

You chose everything, from your height to the size of your nose to your propensity for health or illness; everything!

It is the same with all of your initial conditions in life like your family - with all of their challenges - the time and place where you were born and raised, the circumstances of your town, country, and world.

All of these were specifically selected by you to have the experiences you want in life to learn, grow and creatively expand through living your life.

Embrace yourself. Every part of you is special. You are special on purpose.

YOUR BODY IS A REFLECTION

+++

Ever wonder why you have aches and pains? Why your shoulder hurts or you have acne? Maybe why you have headaches or can't gain weight?

Your body is your most intimate representation of your thoughts, beliefs, and feelings.

If you believe someone in your life is hard to deal with and you feel powerless to do anything about it, that relationship may show up as a pain in your neck, literally.

You create your body constantly, and it expresses your innermost thoughts, beliefs, and feelings. When you feel good, you look better. When you are tired or grumpy, your colleagues can easily see it. Similarly, self-confidence or lack of it shows up for others to see.

If you want to change your body - how it feels or how it looks - start with how you think. What you think about yourself and your place in the world is reflected in your body.

ALLOWING WHAT COMES

+++

Freeing yourself from expectations and allowing what comes to you, runs counter to almost everything many of us were taught growing up.

Planning. Scheduling. Preparing. Anticipating. Creating the 'how' is what we learn to do.

These are all considered good things to do.

But what if you didn't have to? What if you could sit back, be present, and let things come to you? Do you think good things or bad things would come?

That's the crux of the issue, we fear that if we don't plan and schedule, bad things will come.

Where did we learn that? Why is that so ingrained in our thinking and beliefs?

Learning to allow the Universe to handle the 'how' is a challenge for us, but it's ultimately the way the world works, and we can have a much easier life if we relax into allowing.

WHAT IS KNOWING?

+++

There are three levels of certainty. With each level of certainty, you increase the energy, the emotions, and the place from which the energy comes. With increasing levels of certainty, your confidence to create what you want goes up.

The more certain you are of something, the more likely that something is or will be true.

The first level is wanting. At the wanting level is hope and wishes. It's fun to want, but wanting is rarely powerful enough to deliver. You can think of it as a light breeze. It can flitter a few leaves, but barely moving the object of your desire toward you.

The second level is believing. With believing, you usually have evidence that something is true, maybe you heard it from someone you believe. At this level, the energy is stronger, the wind is blowing strong, and whole branches are swinging. With strong feelings behind beliefs, you can achieve great things.

The highest level is knowing. When you know, you don't think to question. This is where we spend most of our life. We know that when we reach for an unlocked door and pull, it will open. We don't hope it will. We know it will.

The power of knowing works in our favor and can work against us. Reaching the knowing when you've started at the wanting level is a very empowering position to be in as you intentionally create your life.

YOU HAVE TOTAL CONTROL

+++

You are in control. In total control.

We have all experienced 'control freaks,' the people who need to plan each step for themselves and everyone around them.

That's not control, but the expression of fear. It is the fear of allowing.

Control is having the confidence to allow things to happen, knowing everything will work out as you wish.

You influence everything in your life with your thoughts, beliefs, and feelings. You are responsible for your life. In that sense, you are in total control.

Exercise control by knowing what you want and allowing it to happen.

YOU SET THE LIMITS

+++

The limits that exist are only the limits we create. We create limits as individuals and as a society. Many of us are comfortable living within the current boundaries we've set for ourselves.

Some see a future unbounded by others. These people believe a way around the limits is possible and make it happen.

We can breakthough any limit or barrier once we set our mind to it.

When the game of basketball was invented in 1891, the idea of a dunk was unimagined. It wasn't until 40 years later when the first dunk was recorded.

Today, even junior high games feature players who are so athletic that they can dunk the basketball.

Our view of what is possible changed in basketball and something that was unimaginable has now become commonplace.

YOU CAN BE ABUNDANT

+++

Regardless of how you define it, you should aspire to be abundant or wealthy.

Many of us have very different definitions of abundance and wealth.

Our definition is having all the resources to allow us to have all the experiences we desire. It has nothing to do with money.

There are limitless resources available in the Universe. It is only our focus on scarcity that makes it appear we have limits.

Our beliefs get in the way of becoming wealthy or having unlimited resources, unlimited abundance. Would you feel guilty having more? Does having more equate to greed?

Most people believe that if they had more, they would be happier, but happiness brings wealth, not the other way around.

Try aligning your thoughts and beliefs with abundance, not with scarcity or lack.

YOU GET WHAT YOU FOCUS ON

+++

You give focus by giving your attention. You do this both intentionally and automatically.

Each moment, we make a choice on what to focus on.

Even though there is so much around us, many of us spend so much time in our head, thinking about things we did or should do.

All of that attention and focus adds up and is reflected back to us in our experiences.

+++

SECTION 3

+++

IT STARTS INSIDE

+++

Everything we see and experience starts inside of us.

Our mind is where everything starts. The outside world reflects our thoughts, beliefs, and feelings.

The world doesn't happen to us. We create the world with others, but always with our consent and involvement. We directly impact all that we see and experience.

The job, relationships, and experiences we have are all based on our thoughts, beliefs, and feelings.

What we see is imagined first. We might not have visualized the exact scenario we see, but the experiences are reflections of our thoughts, beliefs, and feelings.

IT'S ALREADY THERE

+++

There is a process for getting what you want.

1. Decide what you want.

By deciding what you want and having enough energy behind the desire, you create the thing you want.

It is created somewhere in your future.

Your job is to align yourself with the future you want.

You *don't do it* by planning the sequence of events that must happen, *nor do you achieve it by measuring the difference* between what you have and what you want.

2. Be content with what you have, where you are now and convince yourself that you deserve what you want.

By following your intuition and allowing events to come to you, by truly knowing with all your being that you've already created the thing you want and *knowing* without a shadow of doubt that you are on the right path to receive it, you will get what you want.

LEAD WITH YOUR THOUGHTS

+++

It's not what you do, it's *why* you do it that matters.

The reason you do something is the result of your thoughts, beliefs, and feelings.

You can't fake it.

If you want to go to the gym because you hate the way you feel or don't want to be out of shape, you will not have the same level of success as when you go because you love the way you feel and you enjoy being fit.

Focusing on what you want rather than what you don't want will bring you more of what you want.

Embarking on a project knowing you will succeed will more likely lead to success. Likewise, starting off focusing on your fear of failure will more likely lead to the failure you fear.

Your thoughts, beliefs, and feelings are out in front; leading the way and bringing people and experiences to you.

TRUST YOUR FEELINGS

+++

Our feelings arise from our beliefs. They come in response to our interaction with the world based on how we see things.

Feelings are a way to understand our beliefs. If we are feeling happy about most things, we likely have happy beliefs.

If we have feelings of anxiety or fear, our beliefs in that area could be limiting us.

If you wake up in the morning feeling anxious, there is a conflict between your thoughts and beliefs. There is no need to be afraid of anxiety. Instead, learn to welcome the anxiety knowing it is trying to tell you to look at your choices. Don't judge your feelings, but to see them as signposts directing you to look more closely at something causing the anxiety.

Feelings are never invalid. Our reaction to them, and our interpretation of them may be, but the feelings themselves are true.

When we were young, we trusted and followed our feelings so much more than we do as adults. When we are hurt, we cried. When we felt happy, we squealed with joy. When we were curious, we reached out to learn more.

We can learn to trust our feelings again.

YOUR ATTITUDE IS YOUR DESTINATION

+++

We use GPS all the time to get where we want to go. We simply enter the destination and follow the step-by-step instructions, reaching our destination without fail.

You have something just like that in your life.

It is your attitude. Your attitude is a preview of where you are headed. You might as well enter how you are thinking and feeling - your attitude towards things and events - into a GPS because that is where you are headed.

If you are feeling frustrated or upset, that is what you are broadcasting, and you will be attracting more of it into your life.

If you feel appreciative, grateful and contented about where and who you are, more experiences like that will be drawn to you.

WE TRUST OUR BELIEFS

+++

When we read or hear things, and they make sense to us, we tend to believe them.

We usually don't question our beliefs. They are such a part of how we view the world; we don't realize they are there.

For example, the first time you drove to work, you saw the scenery in a completely different light than after years of the same commute. We get used to the same things and don't stop to question them.

When we were young, we reached conclusions without much thought because we heard it from a trusted authority. Many of our beliefs came from our childhood as we experienced life and as our parents or others in society made statements we accepted as true without much thought.

The good news is since we've created our beliefs, we can change them.

We can begin to question our beliefs once we realize they exist.

+++

SECTION 4

+++

A WAY TO BE HAPPY

+++

It sounds simple, but being happy takes some effort. You have to choose to be happy.

If your current situation is not a happy one, you have a choice. You can look around and choose to react unhappily to your surroundings, or you can choose to be happy.

Take one thing, maybe as small as acknowledging that you are able to see or you are able to read and be grateful. Feel a touch of gratitude for something small.

The choice is yours to not fall prey to your current situation, but choose to be happy even if it's just a little bit at a time. It will build on itself.

WHAT ARE YOU ASKING FOR?

+++

When you say you want some 'thing,' it is much more than the 'thing.'

Say you want a new car. It's not just the new car you want. It's the feeling of getting a new car and driving along your favorite road. It's the joy of talking about your new car with friends and family. It's the satisfaction of looking in your garage and seeing the results of your efforts.

When you want something and set it as a desire, the Universe recognizes the larger ask. It recognizes all the emotions and feelings related to the 'thing' you want.

The car is just the symbol of all those emotions and feelings.

Sure, you want the car to drive and to experience. But if you could get those same feelings without the car, would that work as well?

When you think about what you want, think about the whole emotional package behind your ask.

ALL YOUR POWER IS NOW

+++

Our point of impact is now. Everything before now and after now is possible.

The reason now is special is because it is where we are in the moment. It is where we always are. Our conscious focus on now creates our physical reality.

All the possible positions of all atoms can be anywhere and everywhere until we determine with our conscious focus where they should be.

That is when they coalesce in front of us to make what we see real.

We impact our life at every moment. Now is when we exert our power. Now is when we realize our dreams and make new ones.

This is exactly why mindfulness is so special. It helps us appreciate and recognize how powerful we are, in each and every moment.

WAITING IS A GIFT

+++

Waiting is a gift in disguise.

Most of us think about waiting with dread. How many times have we demanded, 'How long is this going to take?'

What is waiting? When does it change from a pause to a wait? Pauses are nice. We get to catch our breath. As a friend of ours pointed out, music without pause is just noise.

Waiting is when we want something to happen, and it doesn't occur when we want it to.

When you are waiting in line at the grocery store, what do you feel? Can you enjoy the moment, or are you focused on the gap and frustration?

The pause is an opportunity to get grounded, be present, and decide what you are going to do next.

We can focus on what is missing, or we can enjoy the pause. When we focus on what is missing, we get more waiting.

SECOND CHOICES

+++

Sometimes, what you hope for doesn't work out.

Maybe you wanted to go to a certain restaurant - had your heart set on a favorite meal - and they were closed.

You can view this as a disappointment, or you can view it as an opportunity.

If you are in your flow, when you are present and open to what's next, the Universe will make things easy. If choices you're making are not in alignment with your flow, then you will get hints - some subtle and others less so - to help you change direction.

Try looking at situations that don't go your way. It might be a signal for you to allow changes to happen. Take advantage of those moments to reconsider and allow for an easier path.

FILTERS AND MAGNETS

+++

Your thoughts, beliefs, and feelings act like filters and magnets and drive what you see and what comes to you.

There is so much happening around us, but we only see a small fraction of it. The part we see is what we focus on.

Like the attractive properties of magnets, our thoughts, beliefs, and feelings attract people and events to us based on their match.

Have you ever tried to have a conversation with someone with opinions in total opposition to yours? It can be painful. No amount of logic or explanation from either of you could ever convince the other.

You've each set up your filters in such a way that nothing they say to you can get through and vice versa.

You might even find yourself attracted to people with conflicting opinions because you unknowingly are looking for arguments.

What you experience passes through a filter that highlights what is aligned with your beliefs and hides what is in conflict with them.

YOUR MICRO-CHOICES

+++

How many choices do you make each day? A dozen? A hundred? A thousand?

There are 86,400 seconds in a day. If you make a choice each waking second, you have about 60,000 opportunities to make a choice. Each of those choices impacts you and your life.

We call them micro-choices.

Each of us gets to choose how we react when waiting in line. We get to accept where we are, or we can wish we were someplace else and miss out on what is right in front of us.

Each of our micro-choices creates our world and color our experiences. We often don't even realize we are thinking and choosing, but we can learn to pay more attention to them.

Our micro-choices are more impactful than our big choices because we are making them all the time.

+++

SECTION 5

+++

DO IT NOW

+++

If you have the impulse to do something, don't put it on a list.

Do it now!

Right now you have the urge, right now you have the creativity and focus.

If you wait and put something on a list, the energy dissipates. The energy becomes more aligned with checking items off your list; more aligned with waiting and delay.

With the power of the entire Universe behind you at the moment, now is the best time to do what you are inspired to do.

THINK ABOUT WHAT, NOT HOW

+++

The Universe has so much more knowledge than we do. We can only remember so much and have limited knowledge of the future and our overall path.

Our job during our lifetime is to choose 'what' we want, then get out of the way. Our job is not to plan or schedule the 'how.' The 'how' is the domain of the Universe.

When we start to define the how, we limit the possibilities for ourselves. The Universe wants us to succeed. It wants to give us what we ask for.

When we say what we want and then say it has to happen a certain way, we get in the way. We send mixed messages; messages with conflicting resolutions that the Universe wants to address equally.

The Universe knows so much more than we do. Give it free rein by asking for 'what' you want and then allowing it to handle the 'how.'

BELIEFS OVER EFFORTS

+++

Many of us grew up learning the 'early bird gets the worm' and we need to 'work hard to get ahead.'

We live in a society that values - even celebrates - the hard worker. Oftentimes, society's role models are people who seem to succeed due to their determination and struggle.

In sports, we talk about the effort an athlete puts in during the off-season. In business, we talk about burning the midnight oil. It's easy to think it's effort that is needed to be successful.

We can achieve results through effort because we believe so intently that our hard work will result in a specific result. Many people go through life this way.

It is our thoughts, beliefs, and feelings that attract people and events into our life. To have what we desire requires us to align our beliefs with our goals.

You will be enormously more productive by attracting your desire with your thoughts, beliefs, and feelings instead of forcing an outcome without first aligning yourself.

TAKE INSPIRED ACTION

+++

Inspired action is something you feel compelled to do, not something you should do or want to do. When you feel inspired to do something, it becomes the simplest and most important thing in the world for you to do.

Getting out of bed, staying up late or skipping meals are all examples of inspired action. It doesn't need to be something really big.

In contrast, an action that is not inspired is like running in place. You can spend a lot of energy and get nowhere. A good example of an uninspired activity is a habit or effort you mindlessly execute.

In writing this book, several ideas for chapters came to us while walking or riding our bicycles. We were doing something else and not focusing on anything in particular, but thoughts showed up that allowed us to add important content to this book.

FILL UP THE SPACE

+++

We fill up our lives. If we wish our lives to be larger, we need to imagine ourselves large enough to fill up the larger space.

We are not talking about physical space, but about how we view ourselves.

In our current circumstances, we've adjusted ourselves and our surroundings to fit. We are just the right size for the things in our life.

We see children who appear destined for greatness. You can sense they are bigger than the space they are in. They are bursting at the seams. They already envision themselves much larger and are busy expanding their experiences and surroundings to match.

If you want to live in a larger house, get a bigger job or in anyway expand your horizons, look inside yourself and see if you can feel big enough to fill up the larger space where you want to be.

If you don't feel that way, ask yourself what's holding you back. You may be surprised at what you find out about yourself.

WE GET IN OUR OWN WAY

+++

Sometimes, life seems hard. We find ourselves struggling to make it through the day.

The Universe doesn't want us to struggle, and we don't want to struggle, so why do we?

It's because we get in our own way. We've been conditioned to expect things in a certain way and build up resistance when things don't work out as we planned.

When we face problems in our life, we sometimes forget to see them as challenges that we can overcome. We then begin to focus on the problem instead of the underlying lessons. We get caught up in reacting and forget that we are the ultimate source of all we experience.

Accepting what is and see how we can influence the present and future rather than stay in our way is a powerful way to view the world.

FAIL IN ORDER TO ALLOW

+++

Sometimes, we have to fail before we can succeed.

When we feel like we've failed, sometimes we let go of the drive, the push, the need to arrive at a specific outcome in a way we've often predetermined.

By letting go, we can finally open up to other possibilities. Possibilities that were invisible only moments before suddenly appear. Most of us get in our own way with details of how we want things to happen.

The sooner we learn to allow insights and events to come to us, the sooner we can live in a world where we don't have to hit a wall or fail to allow the Universe to deliver what we want.

YOU CREATE THE CRISIS

+++

One of our biggest challenges in life is learning not to react to a confrontation. We see or hear something, and we often react automatically. We are taught to confront an issue head-on.

It sounds simple, but the best way out of a situation is not to fight it but to take the path of least resistance. That sounds counter to how we've been raised.

Learn to accept what is happening in the event. Remember that it is a reflection of your thoughts and not some random event that's foisted on you. Think of it as a personal message. Accept it as a valid event and look for the lesson to be learned from the experience.

If you think there is a crisis, then there is one.

ASK WHAT IT MEANS, NOT WHY

+++

When something happens to us, our first reaction usually is to ask, "Why me?"

Why did that guy just cut me off? Why did I miss the meeting? Why is it so busy here?

We wonder why things happen to us. A better question to ask is, "What does it mean to me?"

What are your thoughts, beliefs, and feelings about getting cut off or missing a meeting?

If things in your life are chaotic and crazy, how reflective is that of your mental state?

Take time to examine your thoughts when you can find some quiet space.

PAINT YOUR REALITY

+++

Artists create something that never existed before. They bring their creation to life.

The artist may not always be happy with their work. Some ideas are never started because they seem too ambitious or are beyond the artists' perceived capabilities. Sometimes the fear of what others may think holds them back.

Like an artist, we create our life. Every event in each day is our creation.

We use what is available - both physically and beyond - based on our thoughts, beliefs, and feelings to create days that make us happy.

We also use those same resources to create days in which we are dissatisfied. Sometimes, we barely do either because our fears limit our ability to create what we really want in life.

As the artist of your life, your thoughts, beliefs, and feelings paint the experiences you have during your life. Intentionally focusing on them enables you to create more deliberately.

+++

SECTION 6

+++

LIKE ACTORS IN A PLAY

+++

Do you wonder why our Greater-Self doesn't just reach out to remind us how wonderful we are? Remind us that we are these wonderfully supported beings with no cause to worry? Regularly tell us we are always safe?

Our life is for learning and growing. We live in a world where each of us can experience and explore our creativity. We couldn't if we carried all our combined experiences and memories with us. By focusing on our Active-Self, we are present for the challenges we want to experience.

We are like actors on the stage. As actors, we are totally immersed in the expression of our character.

When we are on stage, we know we are actors. We know the set is not real. If in the play we die or fall in love, we really won't be dead or in love. But for the duration of the play, it is real.

Actors don't need someone in the audience to tell them they are in a play.

In life, we are the actors, and we get to improvise at life. Our Greater-self doesn't want to ruin the experiences we want in life by reminding us we're just in a play.

WE ARE CONDITIONED TO FEAR

+++

Many of us approach life based on fear.

We lock the doors for fear of a robbery or invasion. We buy insurance for fear of illness or accident. We work hard to save money for a rainy day, so we don't end up poor and on the streets. We have so much fear that we don't even notice it.

Fear is a constrictor. It limits our ability to see and paralyzes us from action. It cuts off options and blinds us to possibilities. With fear as our guide, the world is a scary place.

When we see the world through a filter of fear, we justify each of our preventative steps and validate our fears through the people and events we attract.

Yes, there are legitimate things to avoid, but much of what we fear is created in our thoughts and imagination. We fear what *might* happen or what *others think of us*.

We bring more of what we fear into our life when we are fearful.

TO SEE AND NOT JUDGE

+++

You will see things more clearly if you learn not to judge.

We are born to judge. We compare things without any effort. This one is taller. This one tastes better. We judge everything so automatically.

We make choices based on judging one outcome over another. Yet we run into trouble when we judge based on a subjective scale.

This one is good, that one is bad.

When we judge something, we automatically put a label on it. It becomes what we've labeled it. It transforms based on our judgment.

The same is true when we judge ourselves. We judge our thoughts and our actions – sometimes much more critically than necessary.

With practice, we can begin to view things including ourselves as they are - without judgment and labels - and accept them for what they are.

IN SEARCH OF PERFECTION

+++

Have you ever wanted to be perfect or have a situation turn out perfectly?

What is perfection? It implies once it is reached, there is nothing better, no way to improve upon it. Doesn't that depend on the person's perspective?

We've all be in situations where the temperature is just right for us, only to have someone adjust the thermostat to meet their needs.

When we strive for perfection, we miss out on the aspects of life that give it depth and color. We may want perfect kids, perfect homes, perfect friends, but then we miss out on the fun experiences that spontaneously happen from deviations away from our perfect something.

Instead of perfection, think of fabulous.

A fabulous outcome can have good parts and some not so good parts. It is in our acceptance of all the parts that make it fabulous.

IT IS FAIR

+++

We all hear or maybe even say, "That's not fair."

What does it mean to be fair? Does it mean the 'good guy' wins? Does it mean no one cuts in front of you while you're waiting in line?

When we think of fairness, we usually think in terms of things balancing out, like when the bully doesn't win the fight, the rich guy doesn't get richer or the poor guy finally gets his reward.

That's not how it works.

We all get what we believe we want and deserve. Many of us believe we deserve more of what we are getting now.

Unless we change what we believe and focus on changing our life, we will remain on the same path. The rich will get richer, and victims will remain victimized.

It doesn't seem fair, but it is the ultimate in fairness. We all get to choose, and our choices show up in our experiences.

EMPATHY IS ENABLING

+++

When someone is complaining, they are putting their focus on the things they don't want.

Your empathy for another person's complaints creates a reinforcing cycle, which helps keep the person's energy and focus on the very things they don't want.

We can empathize with the person, but not with their complaints.

Instead, we can help them take a more pleasant perspective without aligning with their misery.

HELPING OTHERS

+++

It is not your job to help others.

No one needs your help. Like you, they have access to all the power of the Universe, and like you, they are here in this physical world for specific experiences.

They are working through their challenges just like you.

There is much joy and satisfaction in helping others. That is why we wrote this book and why we want to share our message with others.

We want to help others because we enjoy it.

Here is the difference - trying to help others from a feeling of duty, obligation or guilt will not help you or anyone else.

We are all connected. The best way for each of us to help others is to be true to ourselves.

Everyone benefits when you live *your* life. When you set the example of living a meaningful and fulfilling life, others take encouragement and can see for themselves how they can live theirs.

They can follow your example.

THERE ARE NO COINCIDENCES

+++

When unlikely events occur, we call them lucky (or unlucky). We shake our head at the highly unlikely occurrence or the freak accident, even though so many things had to happen for the event to occur.

There are no coincidences. Life is not preordained. It is driven by the choices we make.

There are valuable lessons in what we see as coincidences.

Have you ever had the experience of thinking about someone in your past and wondering how they're doing, just to see them a short time later?

This is a good example of what we think of as a coincidence, but your thinking and their thinking created the situation.

Try to think of coincidences as signs. Ask yourself what they might mean to you. Are they signals that you should try something different or symbols that you are making great progress along your desired path?

Learn to appreciate 'coincidences' for their messages and remember there are no coincidences.

PROBLEMS OR CHALLENGES?

+++

You can't run away from problems. Without internal changes, the external problems will follow you wherever and whatever you do.

You might not like to hear it, but you set up the problems specifically to work through.

In fact, you might not want to consider them as problems, but as challenges.

Most of us like challenges. We like to solve puzzles, win a game or come in first place in a contest.

We see challenges as something we choose to take on and feel good when we succeed. We put ribbons on our wall and trophies on the mantle.

We tend to see a challenge as a potential for success and a problem as a potential for failure.

Which one would you choose?

IS THERE A CAUSE AND EFFECT?

+++

We live in a society that embraces cause and effect. You work, you get paid. If you commit a crime, you go to jail.

We don't need something to happen in order for something else to happen. There is no cause and effect.

It seems to be the case because we observe it, but that does not necessarily make it so. Our mind is superb at connecting dots, even dots that don't exist or appear to exist.

We anticipate the effect, so it manifests. We see the effect, and then assume that the cause is what happened beforehand.

THE POWER OF NATURE

+++

Do you feel better when you see a sunset, a pretty garden or mountain vista? Do you feel uplifted when spending time out in nature compared to sitting and watching TV or in an office?

We are of nature. We are all intimately connected. Every choice we make and experience we have, impacts everyone and everything.

While everything has consciousness, even the TV and office furniture, the vibrancy of nature is more aligned with who we are. We can more easily become aligned with nature when we are experiencing it.

A month-long hike in the mountains would be fantastic, but it's not for everyone. You can get the same feeling when you walk through the park, or even around the block.

Take time to spend in nature. It can have a very calming effect, especially if you're feeling out of control.

YOU CAN CHOOSE

ABOUT THE AUTHORS

+++

We are a couple of people just like you. In our lifetime, we've had both wonderful experiences, and we've had challenging ones.

A number of years ago, we started a software company in our garage. We struggled like all startups - going through different ideas and business models.

One day, we got a call from a company asking us to build software to replace vending machines. We didn't know anything about vending, but we were in the software business and saw an opportunity to replace vending machines with a little store. It was a great idea; people could just walk into the little store, grab what they wanted from open shelves and coolers and scan it on a self-checkout computer running our software.

It worked. Over just a few years, we installed thousands of these little stores. We had hundreds of millions of dollars of transactions, and our little startup was finally profitable. We grew rapidly and the company was making millions of dollars.

However, as we worked through the challenges of a startup, we were miserable. The work was hard and very stressful. Peter was previously diagnosed with depression, and it was his constant companion throughout this period.

Then, our biggest customer sued us. While it was tough before, now it was horrible. Peter's depression practically smothered him, and it wreaked havoc on our marriage.

Any sleep we could get lasted for maybe two hours at a time. Peter would stress over all the things he had done wrong, and not just with the company, but throughout his whole life. He could only think about how much of a loser he was and how his life was going down the drain.

He didn't know it at the time, but his thoughts, beliefs, and feelings were all "bad" and limiting. He was his own worst enemy - sabotaging himself with every destructive thought.

While it was bad for Peter, it was disastrous for our marriage. I was frustrated with every thing, but especially with Peter. Where did the guy go that I married? No value came from conversation because neither of us could understand the other's perspective.

Then, we got the results from the lawsuit. We lost, big time. Not only did we have to comply with our customer's demand, but they were also leaving us, and we were forced to pay them and our lawyers whatever money we had left.

We had just a few months to go until we ran out of money.

We weren't bankrupt yet, but it was just around the corner. At that point, when we were at our lowest, we chose not to fight, but to let go. We chose to let whatever happen, happen.

That was so hard to do. For ten plus years, we'd been scratching and fighting. Our hard work built the company, and if something didn't happen in our favor, we'd lose everything. We'd have to declare bankruptcy, fire all our employees, and we knew we would view ourselves as failures forever.

Letting go was the best thing we could have done. By letting go, it freed us up.

Letting go took away the all-consuming pressure of figuring out how we were going to get out of the mess and allowed us to focus on what we wanted.

During this time Peter started reading and studying, not about business, but about the power of our mind and the impact of our thoughts, beliefs, and feelings. He read books by Wayne Dyer, Jane Roberts, Hermann Hesse, Ken Wilbur, Wallace Wattles, Steven Hawking, and many others.

He took notes about the readings, including any questions he could think of and let the material sink in over several months, constantly mulling it over. It was a recess from the stress of everything with the company.

One of the lessons was 'You Get What You Focus On.' Peter recognized for a good part of the past few years, that he focused on failure. He focused on all the things that he didn't do right and things that could go wrong. *He focused precisely on what he didn't want to happen.*

While open to new ideas, we are natural skeptics. We both studied science and business and are quite logical. Peter is quick to judge and very good at poking holes in other people's ideas. I have to have proof of something before I believe it and then it has to have some practical value for me to be interested.

The more Peter read about the power of the mind, the more comfortable he became with it. He loved that it was so elegant, simple and logical.

Then one day, it hit him.

The power of my mind is not a theory or something mysterious. It's practical and completely within my reach.

What I think about matters and I can choose what I think about.

That means:

- *I'm in control*

- *I'm not dependent on anyone else.*

- *I can't blame anyone else.*

- *It's all about me.*

- *I'm not a victim.*

- *I'm empowered.*

We were compelled to write and share our lessons from this difficult experience in our lives with others who are beginning to realize there is more to our lives than what we have been told.

We don't have all the answers, and we're learning all the time, but we went from being victims to being winners.

Your Thoughts Matter
and
You Can Choose
Your Thoughts

Beth & Peter Bostwick

www.YouCanChoose.info